PRAYER MADE SIMPLE

David Torkington

All booklets are published
thanks to the generosity of the supporters
of the Catholic Truth Society

If our main preoccupation is prayer it does not mean that we are blind to the political, social or theological problems that beset the world. It means rather that we realise what must come first. Seek first God and his Kingdom of love and then everything else will be given to you.

Prayer is the place where this search begins.

David Torkington

All rights reserved. First published in 2018 by The Incorporated Catholic Truth Society, 40-46 Harleyford Road, London SE11 5AY Tel: 020 7640 0042 Fax: 020 7640 0046 www.ctsbooks.com © 2018 The Incorporated Catholic Truth Society

ISBN 978 1 78469 562 0

Contents

Contents

Chapter 1

The Sun that Never Sets

Some years ago I had dinner with friends in London. When I was leaving their home, I was introduced to their father who was busy digging in the garden. Taken by surprise and not knowing what to say, I asked a rather stupid question. "And what are you doing?" I said. "I do be digging the garden," he replied, glancing at his son as if to say, "Who's your fatuous friend?" Intrigued by his answer I asked a nun who taught Irish in Dublin what was meant by the expression, "I do be digging the garden." She said that it is the English rendering of what is called in Irish, the present continuing tense. It means, "I have been digging the garden, I am digging the garden, and when you stop asking the obvious, I will continue to dig the garden."

There is no such tense in English, but it perfectly expresses the meaning of the Aramaic idiom, as spoken by Jesus, and as emphasised by St John when he said, "God is love" (1 *Jn* 4:8). He was not trying to give a definition of what love is in itself as a Greek philosopher would do, he was describing in his own language that God is loving. That is what he is, and that is what he does, continually.

In order to try and describe the power and magnitude of this love, with which God filled Our Lord at his Resurrection, the early Christians used the symbol of the sun. That is why they called their holy day, Sunday. It not only reminded them of the love of God that filled Christ at his Resurrection, but of that same love, as it was released to fill them on the first Pentecost day. Then finally it was a reminder of how this love was continually being released to fill them on every day.

However, not even the sun could symbolise the real power and energy of God's love. Even if you would join together all the stars in the firmament and multiply the power and energy that they released by as many millions as you like, it would not come anywhere near the power and energy of God's love.

Unlike the sun this infinite loving radiates outward and into all who would receive it, not just during the day, but day and night, to the end of time. If you think that I am indulging in pious hyperbole then think again. No man-made myth, no fairy tale has ever told any story like this. No dreamer has ever dreamed such an incredible truth as this – yet it is the greatest truth ever told by the greatest man who ever lived.

Before the Resurrection Jesus was limited by the physical body into which he freely chose to enter. His choice meant that he could only be in one place at a time, so meeting him would have been as difficult as meeting any major celebrity in our time. But that has all changed now, because the same other-worldly love that raised him out of this world on the first Easter day enabled him to re-enter it on every day. So now he can enter into us as he promised, so that he can make his home in us and we can make our home in him, as he promised at the Last Supper. All this is possible, not in some distant pipe-dream, but here and now in this present moment. That is why Jean Pierre de Caussade, the great Jesuit mystic said, "The present moment contains far more than we have the capacity to receive, for it is full of infinite treasures."

Chapter 2

Where Time Touches Eternity

These infinite treasures are all contained within the love of
God. Then, as this love first strikes a human heart that is
open to receive it, that heart acts like a prism, distributing
that love to every part of the human personality. These
spiritual treasures are not only full of the love we need, but
the virtues too that love generates within us, enabling us to
return this love in kind to God, and then to share what we
have received with others. Jean Pierre de Caussade calls
the here and now the "sacrament of the present moment",
because it is the only moment where time touches eternity.

It is the only moment where the love of God can reach
out to us and we can reach out to him, to begin and to
continue the journey for which every human being yearns
deep down within them. It is the journey to the ultimate
mystical marriage for which we all yearn, where our love
and the love of Christ become one, in the Three in One,
and to all eternity. This is what we call the 'Good News'
because it is the best possible news that anyone can ever
hear. But the bad news is that the infinite love that is
continually available to us is different from all other forms

of energy, because love cannot be forced. We know this from our own experience as human beings. No matter how we might love someone or no matter how much they might love us, if that love is not welcome, if it is not received and reciprocated, then it will have no effect at all no matter how powerful it may be.

It is the same with God's love. That is why from the very beginning the first question asked by the great saints and mystics is not, "How do we love God?" but, "How do we freely choose to turn and open ourselves to receive his love?" It is only then that his love can begin to enter into our love in such a way that it can suffuse and surcharge our human loving with the divine.

Then it can begin the ascent, in, with and through Christ, through whom this love is given, to contemplate the Father in whom our final destiny is brought to perfection. But, and there always seems to be a 'but' when we hear good news; if we do nothing to try to receive God's love then nothing will happen except that instead of going forwards in the spiritual life we will go steadily backwards.

Chapter 3

The Spiritual Escalator

Making the spiritual ascent to God is rather like trying to run up a downward escalator. The moment you stop moving steadily forwards is the moment when you start moving steadily downward. A hermit once said that they did not fear a precipice, for only a fool would fall over it. It is the steady downward slope that we should fear in the spiritual life.

Going steadily forwards means finding daily time to do what St Peter told his listeners to do when he was the first to announce the Good News that God's love had just been unleashed on the first Pentecost day. He told them to keep turning and opening themselves to God's love every moment of their lives. Speaking to them in languages they could understand, he used the word 'repent'. In Hebrew there is no such word for someone who has repented, but only for someone who is repenting. It is a continuous ongoing process that pertains to the very essence of the Christian life. This repenting or this turning and opening oneself to receive the love of God has to be learnt, and the place where it is learnt has traditionally been called prayer. That is why there is nothing more important in our lives than prayer, because without it we cannot receive the only love that can make us sufficiently perfect to enter into the life of the Three in One to which we have been called. That is why St Teresa of Avila said, "There is only one way to perfection and that is to pray; if anyone points in another direction then they are deceiving you." There is nothing therefore more important than prayer.

When human beings love their love is both physical and spiritual, but as God has no body he loves with his spirit alone. As a mark of respect we have come to call his love the Holy Spirit. As we keep turning and opening ourselves to receive the Holy Spirit in prayer, he continually draws us up like a supernatural magnet into Christ: then, in, with and through him into the life of the Three in One, to contemplate and enjoy the Father's love for all eternity.

Chapter 4

It's All in the Trying

Many years ago I was privileged to attend a retreat given by Cardinal Hume. He first quoted and then slightly modified the definition of prayer given in what used to be called the old penny Catechism. "Prayer," he said is "trying to raise the heart and mind to God." The word he introduced to the old definition was "trying", to emphasise that the essence of prayer is all in the trying.

The quality of our prayer is ultimately determined by the quality of our endeavour. It was for this reason that the great mystic and mother, Blessed Angela of Foligno said that prayer is, "The School of Divine Love". In other words, it is the place where we learn how to love God by daily trying to raise our hearts and minds to him. I intend to introduce you to the different means and methods that tradition has given us to help us to keep trying to turn and open our minds and hearts to God in this little series, but first let me say this. There are no perfect means to help us keep trying to raise the heart and mind to God, just different means. What helps you at the beginning, may not help you later on. What helps you in the morning may not help you in the evening. What helps me, might not help you. Remember the famous words of Dom John Chapman, "Pray as you can and not as you can't." The acid test is, does this means of prayer help me to keep trying to keep raising my heart and mind to God?

One thing I will promise will happen when you seriously set aside some daily space and time for prayer. You will find that no matter what means of prayer you choose to use, you will be deluged by distractions. After a few weeks of distractions and temptations buzzing around in the head like a hornet's nest, many people come to the conclusion that they cannot pray. They then tend to pack up giving a special time for prayer and only turn to God in extremis when they are in trouble. Here is the secret of prayer that has to be learned from the outset. The very distractions that you think are preventing you from praying are the very means that enable you to pray. That is why St Teresa of Avila said that you cannot pray without them. Each time you turn away from a distraction to turn back to God, you are in fact performing an act of selflessness; you are saying no, to self and yes, to God. If in fifteen minutes you have a hundred distractions, it means that one hundred times you have made one hundred acts of selflessness. Gradually, if you continue to do this day after day, then acts of selflessness lead to a habit of selflessness that helps you to pray better and better. That is why Blessed Angela of Foligno said that prayer is the School of Divine Love where loving is learnt by practising selfless loving.

If you have many distractions and you keep turning away from them, then you will get straight As when the examination comes round. If, however, you only have two – one is dreaming about where you are going for your next summer holiday and the next is worrying about how to get the money to get there, then that is a different matter.

Let us suppose that when you settle down to pray you fall asleep. Is that prayer? No. On the other hand, let us suppose that the moment you are preparing to pray you are swept up into an ecstasy. Is that prayer? No. In the first case you were doing nothing, and in the second case God was doing everything. Strictly speaking you were not praying at all in either case. Prayer is what happens between the sleep and the ecstasy where you are continually trying to raise your heart and mind to God, and in so doing learning how to love in the School of Divine Love.

Chapter 5

It is in Giving that we Receive

Blessed Angela calls prayer the School of Divine Love, not just because it is the place where the selflessness that leads to love is learnt, but for something further. In the words of St Francis of Assisi, it is in giving that we receive. In other words, as we try to give ourselves to God in prayer he gives himself to us. In our very endeavour to turn away from distractions in order to raise our hearts and minds to God, our endeavour becomes the channel through which our love rises to God and God's love descends into us. It is only then, as our weak human love is suffused and surcharged by the divine that we can begin to love God like never before. Then we can begin to observe the new commandment that Jesus taught us, which is to love God with our whole heart and mind, with our whole body and soul.

At first glance it might be thought that this is not a new commandment, but the old commandment that the Jews in the Old Testament were taught. Yes, it was given to the Jews in the Old Testament, but they could never observe it as God wanted them to until Jesus came to show them how.

Remember when St Peter told the crowd that the love of God promised in the Old Testament was on that very day being unleashed upon all, he told them to repent or to turn and open their hearts and minds to receive it. However, he told them to do something else too. He told them to be baptised, to undergo the new initiation ceremony. This initiation would not so much mark their entrance into a new organisation, institution or religion, but their entrance into a person, the person of Jesus himself, now risen and glorified.

So, now when they were told to continue repenting, trying to raise their hearts and minds to God, they would do it in him. But that is not all, for the same Holy Spirit whom he sent would so enter into their prayer that now they would be able to pray with him, and through him, to the Father who sent him in the first place.

The daily battle against distractions now takes on a new meaning, for now it enables us to participate in Christ's death and Resurrection: by daily dying each time we say 'no' to self, and 'yes' to God. Once prayer is seen in this context then what was originally seen as a pointless activity can be seen as the most important activity that we could ever perform. This book is called *Prayer Made Simple* but that does not mean that it is easy. After all, who would expect that learning the most important thing that any human being can learn would be easy? Learning to love in the School of Divine Love may not be easy, but it is the most important thing that we can learn, not just for our happiness on earth, but for our ultimate happiness hereafter.

The selflessness learnt in prayer helps us outside of prayer too, as the habit of selflessness enables us to love others, our families, our husbands and wives, our children and others too who have need of our love. Now we see that the second of the new commandments becomes possible. It is so often misquoted as commanding us to love others as ourselves. I am afraid that is the teaching of the Old Testament. The second of the new commandments, as given to us by Jesus himself, is to "love one another; just as I have loved you" (*Jn* 13:34). This can only become possible when, as we try to love him in prayer, our endeavour becomes the channel that enables his love to enter into us and into our loving, enabling him to love others through us.

Chapter 6

The Quality of our Endeavour

Our self-love is so deeply rooted within us that it takes a long time and a long spiritual journey trying to practise the two new commandments before practice comes anywhere near being perfect. But in time the more we try the more the Father and the Son will begin to make their home ever more deeply within us, as Jesus promised at the Last Supper (*Jn* 14:21-24). Then the love that binds the Father and the Son together will begin to overflow into our love, suffusing it with the divine. Gradually we will find that we will be able to love God as never before, and love others too as Christ himself loves us.

When Our Lady turned and raised her heart and mind to God and said, "Yes", the Holy Spirit was able to conceive Christ within her immediately, because in her there were no obstacles to his grace. Her Immaculate Conception meant that the sin and selfishness that is in us was never in her, so there was nothing to prevent the instantaneous conception of Jesus within her. Because we are not immaculately conceived, what happened to her instantly can only happen to us gradually, and only if we keep saying, "no" to self, and "yes" to God, in days or rather in years, practising loving in the School of Divine Love. As this loving is being learnt, the love of God begins to do in us what was done in Mary, as the obstacles that were never in her are gradually purified away by the fire of the Holy Spirit, who is at work within us.

Eventually, as Christ is born again in us, the love received from him overflows outside the special times set aside for prayer to irrigate everything that we say and do in the rest of our lives. In this way we gradually begin to practise the *prayer without ceasing*, as every moment of our day becomes the time and place where we try to love God in all we say and do, and most especially through those we try to love.

The sacrifices involved in doing this become the offerings that we take with us to Mass. This is the moment when, with the rest of the Christian community we offer up to God, in, with and through Christ all the sacrifices that we have made as we tried to pray without ceasing throughout the previous week. These sacrifices added to the great sacrifice of Christ himself, enable God to fill us with his love in return, for it is indeed in giving that we receive.

It is important to emphasise that the capacity to receive his love in return will not just be determined by the quality of the love that we try to generate once we have gone into the church, but by the quality of the love that we have generated in the prayers, the good works, and the sacrifices that we have made during the previous week. These are the sacrifices that when offered at Mass determine the measure of the love that we will receive in return.

It is this love that will enable us to go out and make the rest of our lives into the Mass. For, as the great Jesuit theologian Karl Rahner put it: "The Mass should so form us that the whole of our lives becomes the Mass, the place where we continually offer ourselves through Christ to the Father."

I have repeatedly used the word 'trying' because God will ultimately judge our prayer by no other standard than by the quality of our endeavour, not by how successful we might think our prayer has been. In the same way God will eventually judge our whole life, not by what we or others might think we have achieved, but by how best we have tried. The French philosopher Simone Weil put it this way: "A person is no more than the quality of their endeavour." That is how God will judge us, always bearing in mind "the slings and arrows of outrageous fortune" visited upon a person by the nature and nurture that is not of their choosing.

One day when or if we get to heaven, we will see people whom we looked down on in this life rewarded far more generously than we would have expected, because their best endeavour was far greater than ours. In heaven a person is rewarded for what they have achieved, despite the odds that were arrayed against them. Those who were given so much and achieved so little will remember with regret the words of the Gospel warning that to those who are given much, much will be expected. In heaven, unlike on earth, there will be a hierarchy of holiness and one's place in this hierarchy will be determined by how best we tried, balanced against what we were given.

Chapter 7

From Here to Eternity

When his disciples asked him how to pray, Jesus gave them the "Our Father". These two words are the key to understanding the basic context and direction of all Christian prayer. The first word puts us in the right context which is in Christ. That is where we pray, always in him, and with him to give glory to God.

Many years ago I used to run a retreat and conference centre in London. As I had to run the place on a shoe string I tried to do as many of the odd jobs myself to save money. But I always had to call in the plumber when the drains were blocked. One day when he was having his lunch I went to look inside his tool box to see if I could find the tool that he used to save me calling him again. It was then that I saw these words written in Latin inside the lid: *Ad majorem Dei gloriam* (All for the honour and glory of God). This was what he prayed and did each day as it has been for all sincerely practising Christians from the very beginning, as it was for Jesus himself.

When in the first century the martyr St Justin was writing about the celebration of the Mass, he said that at the end of the Eucharistic prayer when the priest said, "Through him, with him, in him, in the unity of the Holy Spirit all glory and honour is yours almighty Father, for ever and ever," the "Amen" of the faithful was so loud that it nearly raised the roof. Their "Amen" was so strong, so loud and so vibrant because the priest was not just summing up the offering they were making at that Mass, but the offering they were making with every fibre of their being at every moment of their lives, in and through all they said and did each day. For all they said and did was for his honour and glory, and in living for God and his glory they forgot themselves.

At a school retreat I attended many years ago, the retreat master began by asking us when we last felt really happy. One boy said it was when fishing with his dad, another playing football, another when enjoying a film with his friends. A girl said it was when she was helping her mother with her shopping or spending time alone with her boyfriend, and so the examples multiplied. When we were asked what all these different experiences had in common, we all came to see that we were so lost in what we were doing that we forgot ourselves, at least for a time.

The same thing happens when we learn how to live for God, at least for a time. That is why God teaches through Jesus how to live for him and for him alone, for his honour and glory, not our own. The truth of the matter is our puny efforts do not add one jot or iota to the happiness of God. He did not create us for his pleasure or satisfaction but for our own. The incredible mystery of God's love is that he does not actually need us to praise him and give him all honour and glory; he teaches us to do this because it is in doing this that we are taken out of ourselves to centre our attention on him, and to receive what he gives in return.

This is the highest form of human action that eventually leads to moments of great happiness on earth and to eternal, unending happiness in heaven. This action can begin here and now in this present moment if we are ready and able to set out on the journey that leads from here to eternity. The love of God that we come to experience in this journey is the by-product of losing ourselves in him.

Chapter 8

Journey's End

Our journey's end is not so much to a place, but to a person, to the One who wants us to call him Father, and the place to which we are going is home.

You might have looked at that moving clip on *YouTube* when a convert from Islam told how, on reading the Gospels to see what the prophet Jesus had to say about Allah, he discovered something that changed his life. He discovered that Allah was not a distant God, but a tender loving father, his father, even his dad. *Abba* was the word Jesus used and told others to use when speaking to him. It is the word still used by young Arabic people today to address their fathers.

Born Christians too often take for granted the world-shaking truth of why Jesus came, and the news he came to share with us. He is our brother and we have the same father, the dad who has given us new life and a temporary home with him in this life, until we are ready for the home he has prepared for us in the next. This home that he came from and to which he returned, will one day be our home too. It is here that we will eternally share in the utter peace, joy and bliss of going out of ourselves through love into endless ecstasy. We will share this experience too, not just with Jesus, but with all those we have loved on earth, but purified of all the human weaknesses that once prevented us from loving them as we would have wished. This is what the first Christians called the Good News, the news that Jesus came to bring us. His message was that God is not just love, but that he is loving us all the time and that he loves us not just as a father, but as a dad.

In the Old Testament God tended to be a rather distant father, but Jesus taught that he is far more than that. He is a loving, tender father, a dad, because he not only loves us, but he wants to communicate his own inner life to us. In that life is the source and origin of every form of love that can be found on earth, and every form of love that a person needs to become fully complete and mature, ripe and ready, not just for marriage with another human being, but with God. Jesus did not just tell people about this love, he showed them this love embodied in himself, made tangible through all he said and did while he was on earth, through his tender loving human personality. When he was glorified he was still the same man as before with all the human feelings and affections that he had on earth, but now they are brought to perfection enabling him to love us even more deeply and more tenderly than before.

Christ teaches us to call God, father, when we pray, because this is precisely what he is to us now. The actual word Jesus uses is even more telling than the translation to which we have become accustomed. He did not in fact use the word that is the equivalent to our word, father, instead he chose the word *Abba*. This Aramaic word actually means daddy, or at least the word daddy is the closest we can get to the original meaning. Christ's use of this familiar and homely pet name was not only new, it would also have been shocking to his fellow Jews. I do not mean that God was never referred to as father before, he was in fact called father thirteen times in the Old Testament. However, each time the word was used, it was as another word for creator. In other words, God was a father insofar as he was responsible for his own handicraft, in the sense that we would say Michelangelo was the father of his statue Moses because he carved it, or Herodotus was the father of history, because he created the literary genre.

The traditional word for father, then, was already loaded with a meaning that Jesus wished to supersede. The word *Abba* or daddy, or its equivalent in any language, can mean only one thing. What is a daddy? Who is a daddy, but one who communicates his life to his children? There can be no misunderstanding as to what is meant by this word. The nuance is crucial for the new understanding that Jesus wished to convey about God.

God is now no longer to be understood merely as our Father, the One who created us, but the One who chooses to share his own life with us. This one word sums up the fullness of the Gospel message. If we only allow the same Spirit of love that entered into the life of Jesus to enter into our lives too, then we will be able to share not only in his life, but also in his action, in his love of the Father and in the Father's love of him.

If this truth is to change our lives, which it can, then it must be translated into experience. This can only happen if we put aside the time daily, to create the quality space and time in which to allow God to become a loving father to us and then respond to him as best we can.

Chapter 9

The Journey Begins

I would like to share with you a memory jog or a mnemonic to remind you of the essential ingredients of the daily prayer that we should make each day. When his disciples first asked him how to pray, Jesus gave them the "Our Father".

Try to use every letter of the two words, "Our Father" as a reminder of the essential ingredients of all authentic Christian prayer. Use the letters O-U-R as a reminder of the three essential features of Morning Prayer. The letter O would be a reminder to say the morning offering in one form or another. The letter U would be a reminder that as we make this prayer, we are uniting ourselves with Christ and with all who are in him. Then the letter R would be a reminder to review the coming day, resolving to do all and everything for the honour and glory of God.

Every letter of the word "Father" could be used too, as a reminder of how to pray during the day at a time set aside for that purpose. The letter F will be a reminder to make an act of faith. Once we have briefly meditated on what God has done for us, and is continuing to do for us, it is time to make our response. Use the remaining letters of the words "Our Father", accordingly. The letter A stands for the word abandonment, T for thanksgiving, H for Holy Communion, E for examination of conscience, and finally R for repentance. In this way the words "Our Father" can become a memory jog that we can carry with us at all times to which we can turn whenever there is an opportunity to help transform our day into the *prayer without ceasing*. To help beginners, and are we not all beginners, I have included nine prayers which I have added to the last chapters of this book.

It is a good idea to begin daily prayer by trying to visualise our Risen Lord, as he is now, in the act of loving, in the act of sending out the inner mystical loving that revolves endlessly between the Father and the Son. The icon of the transfigured Christ helps me to do this now, as the picture of the Sacred Heart helped me before, but there are other similar images that can do the same. Above all remember everything will ultimately depend on our perseverance.

Chapter 10

O:
The Morning Offering

On the day when Pope Benedict first used the Internet to tweet, he was asked by one of his respondents how married people living such busy lives could find time for prayer? He replied, "By offering everything that is said and done each day to God." First thoughts on waking each morning, he said, should be to offer the forthcoming day to him. It was my mother who first taught me to say the morning offering. She told me that by offering all that I said and did to God in the day ahead of me I would be able to transform ordinary little things into precious gifts for God, just as Rumpelstiltskin had turned straw into gold.

My mother taught me to say my morning offering the moment I woke in the morning. But above all she showed me how to put it into practice by her own example. It was not the little things that I noticed at first, but the big sacrifices that she made, that even I noticed. Like that terrible moment in her life when her own precious son, my brother, was killed at the age of only twenty-two. It was with the help of her spiritual director, Abbot Williams, that she gradually learnt to accept his death, as Mary did as she stood at the foot of the cross. Lessons learnt in such moments are never forgotten. They indelibly stain the memory and determine the way you think and act for the rest of your life, for better or for worse.

In my mother's case it was for better not worse, as it was for Mary. For both of them it meant that through their terrible ordeal, their motherhood had somehow been refined and deepened to the benefit of other children who looked to them for the motherly love that was always given without measure. I for one know this because I experienced it for myself, and still do. My morning offering always reminds me of my mother for it was she who first taught me how to make it. It reminds me of the other Mother too, who inspired her and who was given to us all by Jesus as he died on the cross. So this is the time in my morning prayer when I say a Hail Mary to ask her to help me today, as I try to offer all I say and do to God the Father through her son, Jesus.

I always try to remember my mother's terrible loss and to pray for her as well as for my brother.

When our family went to Mass each Sunday, they saw their mother totally absorbed in what they took all too easily for granted. Their selfishness meant that they had too little to offer, while she was offering a thousand and one acts of self-sacrifice made for them during the previous week.

This meant that she received to the measure of her giving. Without any formal theological education, she discovered for herself that the Mass is not only a sacrifice, the place where we offer ourselves, in, with and through Christ to the Father, but something more. It is also a sacred sacrificial meal where we receive the love that he is endlessly pouring out, onto and into all who are open to receive it, through daily sacrificial giving.

It was here that she received the help and strength she needed to go on selflessly giving in the forthcoming week for the family that she loved so much. Each day she reminded herself of this, her sacred calling, by making her morning offering, as her recusant ancestors had done for hundreds of years before her. If ever I forgot to say mine she used to remind me that the Curé d'Ars would say, "All that we do without offering it to God, is wasted," and he was right.

Chapter 11

U:
In Union with the Mystical Body

It was my mother who first taught me something so profound that I would never forget. She said that even though I may make my morning offering alone by the side of my bed, I was not alone. Nor would I be alone even if I became a hermit and lived in the middle of some distant desert, or a prisoner locked up in solitary confinement at the other side of the world. My prayer would always be made in, with and through Jesus, and so with all other living Christians wherever they are.

She quoted the "Our Father" to press her point home. When we petition the Father, we do not petition him for ourselves alone as the prayer makes abundantly clear. It says, "Give *us* this day our daily bread and forgive *us* our trespasses as we forgive those who trespass against *us*, and lead *us* not into temptation, but deliver *us* from evil. Amen." She taught me further that praying to the Father in Jesus also means praying with all those who have died and who are now alive again in him. That means with

Mary and Joseph, with St Peter and St Paul, St Dominic and St Francis, with St Catherine of Siena, St Teresa of Avila and St Thérèse of Lisieux, and all the other great saints and mystics.

It also means praying for, with and to all my own relatives and friends both living and dead who are alive again in him. She especially taught me to pray for the Holy Souls, those who have died but who are not yet fully prepared to be united with the Risen One for the sins and the fruits of their sins that keep them at bay until they are purified away. Unlike things cannot be united, so we must be cleansed either in this life or in the next from all that prevents us from having full union with Jesus, before that which we desire more than anything else can take place.

My mother not only taught me to pray for the Holy Souls but to them too. She also told me that this was the perfect opportunity to pray for others, especially those who have asked me to pray for them. She said when you hear about people who are suffering all over the world, on the radio, the television or in the newspaper, you can reach out to them through prayer, because prayer is not limited by space and time as we are.

One morning a lay brother, thinking that Padre Pio was out, burst into his room as he was lost in prayer. The saint dismissed his apologies with the words, "I was only praying for a happy death for my father." "But your father died two years ago," the brother said, looking rather surprised. Padre Pio looked at him in disbelief.

"I know he did!" Prayer is not limited by the laws of space and time and that is why, although St Thérèse of Lisieux never left her Carmelite monastery, she was made patroness of the missions.

Some years ago I went to see an opera at Covent Garden by John Tavener called *Thérèse*. Through the sublime music and profound words, the composer showed how on her deathbed her prayer could reach forward to help soldiers who were to suffer in the First World War and backwards to those who had suffered in the past, as well as to a condemned murderer in the present that he may repent before he was executed, and this prayer was answered.

The wonderful thing about praying for others at this time of the day, is that they can be included in the prayer that is transposed into action for the rest of our day, as we try to offer up all we say and do for the honour and glory of God.

Chapter 12

R:
Reviewing the Day Ahead

Despite what I have just said, it must be emphasised that the morning offering is not a magic formula. It does not automatically transform the forthcoming day, and that is why something further is required. After making the morning offering, spend a few minutes reviewing the day ahead, making a few resolutions that would enable you to try to consecrate every moment of the day to loving God. It might be in pausing for brief moments of prayer during the day, as the early Christians did, but also in doing humdrum tasks that we keep putting off, like changing the sheets on the bed, putting air into the car tyres, defrosting the freezer or something that is more important.

There is always that friend or relative who is sick or in need, whom we should telephone, or write to, or even visit for a few minutes. Alternatively, perhaps we should make a resolution to apologise to one of the family, a friend, or someone at work for the way we behaved towards them the previous day. It is very difficult to stand up for someone who has been abused by authority at work, or elsewhere, or to speak the truth when no one wants to hear it, or to make a stand for what we know is right. But nevertheless, these are some of the more important things that could occupy our minds as part of Morning Prayer.

Perhaps we could end with the most important resolution of all, to try and make the forthcoming day a day when we try as best we can to enable God's love to draw us up, not just into the life of Christ, but into his priestly action. In this way, every day is a day in which we spend every single moment trying to observe the new commandments, firstly by loving God, and then by loving him in the neighbour in need, just as Jesus did.

The spirituality of the Middle Ages was deeply influenced by a story that everybody knew from their childhood. It was the story of a Roman soldier and of his act of compassion for a fellow human being. The Roman soldier was later to become St Martin, Bishop of Tours who was born at the beginning of the fourth century. He was still only a catechumen when, on a cold winter's night, he cut his cloak in half to clothe a half-naked man who was starving to death outside the city gate. When the story was told that the poor man was in fact Christ, its impact was immense and lasting.

Pope Francis had a similar experience of the poor when he became a bishop. He learnt something deep and profound that he has since tried to convey to others. On the vigil of Pentecost he asked his audience a rhetorical question, "Do you give alms to the poor?" Receiving the expected answer, he said, "Very good, but when you give alms to the poor, do you look them in the eye, do you touch their hands?" We are not changed just by giving, but by the way in which we give. This is the insight that Pope Francis discovered for himself. It is in the way in which we give to the poor that we can discover Christ in them, and through this experience be changed ourselves, as others have been changed before us.

One of the most important truths of the spiritual life that we neglect at our peril is that we will not ultimately be judged by the wonderful feelings that we have experienced in prayer. We will not be asked how many ecstasies we have had or even how many miracles we have worked, or people we have healed, but how we have served God in the neighbour in need. But if we fail to do this, then we will be condemned to hear these frightening words, "Go away from me…for I was hungry and you never gave me food" (*Mt* 25:41-46).

The morning offering and its implementation then, is not just a nice, pious practice for those who have the time to do it, but something on which our ultimate destination depends. It is the place where the whole of the forthcoming day is dedicated to loving God through a continual process of prayer, self-sacrifice and the service of others. In this way all that is said, done and suffered, all that is enjoyed and celebrated, is offered in, through and with Jesus to our common Father. This is the new worship "in spirit and truth" (*Jn* 4:24), that Jesus promised to the Samaritan woman and is put into practice. We are called to take part in the priestly action of Jesus every moment of every day of our lives.

The great liturgical scholar Joseph Jungmann put it this way: "Christ does not offer alone, his people are joined to him and offer with him and through him. Indeed, they are absorbed into him and form one body with him by the Holy Spirit who lives in all."

Chapter 13

F:
Faith in Our Risen Lord

Always begin prayer with a profession of faith. I do not mean by reciting some traditional formula of faith, or even professing belief in every article of the Creed or in every dogma that the Church teaches. There is a time and place for that. However this is the time for something else. Our faith is not firstly a belief in a body of truths, but in a body full of love that was filled to overflowing on the first Easter day.

Ever since the first Pentecost day, God's love has been pouring out of Jesus and into all who freely choose to receive it, to draw them into the fullness of life that is fully embodied in his risen body, sometimes called his Mystical Body. It is here alone that we are all destined to "live and move and have our being" (*Ac* 17:28 *KJV*), and experience something of the ecstatic bliss that Jesus experiences now and to all eternity. This is another reason why the fish became a symbol of a Christian in the early Church. They came to see and understand that the love of God was for them what the sea is for the fish, the living environment outside of which they could not exist. St Augustine takes this analogy one step further, substituting a living sponge for the fish to show that we are not only surrounded at all times by the love of God, but are penetrated through and through by his all-pervading presence. This loving presence is the supernatural environment in which we can grow, becoming ever more perfect Christ-like human beings. But even this profound analogy of the sponge is surpassed by St Gregory of Nyssa. He explains that like all love, the love of God that possesses us also acts like a powerful magnetic force. It draws us relentlessly back towards God our Father and to the place where we were first conceived, and to where we will enjoy our ultimate destination.

All this takes place not in a vague void or vacuum, but within us because, as the Gospels make clear, the Kingdom of God is within us. So, when you make your act of faith in the love of God, realise why his love is being poured out now, and how it is re-making and moulding you from the inside into the image and likeness of Christ through whom it is being sent. Realise too how the love that is transforming you is simultaneously drawing you towards the endless ecstatic bliss of experiencing love without measure and to all eternity. This profound mystical journey will continue as long as you continue to remain open and receptive each day to receiving it though the selflessness learnt in practising daily prayer and good works. When we have made our act of faith slowly and prayerfully, mulling over what it means, reflecting and ruminating on all that has been said, it is time to pause in contemplative stillness. Gradually, in time, a sublime realisation will begin to stir in the utmost depth of your being. For once this act of faith has been reflected on and understood, we will inevitably be inspired to make another act. This time, it is an act of total abandonment to God through Jesus.

What other response could we possibly make? If this is asking too much, then sadly it means that we have become wedded to a purely nominal faith that leads us to do no more than the bare minimum. It means that we have become completely oblivious to God's ongoing plan, to sweep us up here and now into the man Dom Eugene Boylan called "This Tremendous Lover". For it is here, even in this life, that he wants us to experience something of the ecstatic bliss that will be ours to eternity in the next.

Chapter 14

A:
Abandonment

Although we do not know a hundred and one things that Jesus did in the hidden years, we do know the most important things that he did. We know when he prayed, where he prayed and how he prayed, continually abandoning himself to his Father. We know that he prayed first thing in the morning to consecrate his day to God, we even know some of the prayers and some of the psalms that he would have used for that purpose. We know that he would have prayed last thing at night too, and some of the prayers and psalms to which he would have turned. He would have gone to the synagogue each day, to say a prayer called the *Shema*. For the Jews, and therefore for Jesus too, this prayer embodied within it a total abandonment to God by promising to love him with "all your heart, with all your soul, and with all your strength," as they were commanded to do, as the first and greatest of all the commandments (*Dt* 6:5). This prayer was said three times each day in the synagogue, at the third, the sixth, and the ninth hour. If for whatever reason a good Jew was prevented from doing this then at those same times he would stop his work or his journey, or rise from his sick bed to say the prayer that was meant to dedicate every moment of every day to God.

They also said another prayer whenever they came together for meals, to thank God not just for the food on the table, but for land that was given them to provide for it. They thanked him too for all he did for them in the past, was doing for them now, and had promised to do for them in the future. This prayer was called the *Berakah*, the prototype for what we now call the Canon of the Mass.

The times set aside for the recitation of the daily *Shema* were not arbitrary, for it was at these times that the sacrifices were being made in the Temple at Jerusalem. When the first Christians continued to pray at these times they were taught that now the Old Temple was no more. They were in future to offer themselves in the New Temple which was Christ. In order to remind them that in doing this they were uniting themselves to his sacrifice, they were encouraged to reflect on his condemnation to death at nine in the morning, to remember his crucifixion at twelve and his death at three o'clock. This would help them to continually participate in his sacrificial life and death, abandoning themselves to the Father through him.

Chapter 15

T:
<u>T</u>hanksgiving

If we only thank God for what we manage to get out of him or for what he has done for us, then we have hardly begun to thank him as we should. He should be thanked for being God, for being goodness, justice, truth and beauty, for displaying his inner glory in the glory of creation that surrounds us, and for the masterpiece of creation in and through whom we are drawn up to share in his own inner life and love.

When I first began to thank God for being God, it was as if I was raised beyond myself and into God's world, if only for a brief moment when my prayer life reached higher peaks than ever before. Try this little experiment. When you have thanked God for what he has done for you, start thanking him for what he is and what he does for everyone, just by being what he is. Take your favourite prayer or hymn of thanksgiving or praise, like the Gloria from the liturgy for instance. Recite it slowly and prayerfully and you will find you are taken out of yourself, out of your world and into God's world where you praise him, thank him and give him glory with all those who have learned to thank God just for being God. You will find that the further you enter into his world, the more you will forget yourself and the world where you only thanked him for what you get out of him. Then you will come alive, more alive than ever before, if only for a time in the world where you want to be for all time.

Thanking God for being God leads into the heights of prayer where thanksgiving leads to praise, and praise to glorifying God. Glorifying God leads to adoration, when we just want to gaze upon him with a profound reverence and awe that takes us out of ourselves if only for a time into brief moments of rapturous bliss.

Without us realising fully what has been happening, our thanksgiving, praising, glorifying and adoring has paved the way for our love to enter into God and his love to enter into us in a way and on a level that has not happened in quite the same way before. Our very perseverance in giving glory to God gradually becomes our personal 'Jacob's ladder' that enables our love to rise to him, and his love to descend into us, to make his home within us, and for us to make our home in him.

Chapter 16

H:
<u>H</u>oly Communion

When Jesus foretold that he would become the Bread of Life, he was not only referring to his presence in the Eucharist, but much more. He was referring to his daily, moment by moment and ongoing presence, as the Bread of Life in the lives of his followers. In short, he would become the staple diet of their daily spiritual lives too. In modern times, it might be possible to interpret the words in the Lord's Prayer, "Give us this day our daily bread," as referring to daily Mass, but in ancient times when daily Mass was unknown and would remain virtually unknown for over a thousand years or more, it referred to the daily Bread of Life that was Christ himself. He is prepared and poised at every moment to nourish us with this spiritual food which is nothing other than his own life and love, just as he fed our spiritual forebears in the desert (*Jn* 6).

The letter H in the mnemonic is a reminder to pause in our daily prayer in silent contemplation to reflect on the Holy Communion that is taking place within us, disseminating the mystical food without which we would languish and die. It is a time to ruminate on and relish the profound mysteries that are at work deep down within us, and to digest and assimilate their sublime meaning and importance for us now and for our future. It is time too, to allow these truths to percolate through, to penetrate our hearts and minds, and then gaze for as long as possible at the indescribable mysteries that Jesus came to share with us. This is the time for us to speak with him and to share with him our most secret thoughts and desires.

At the Last Supper when Jesus spoke about these sublime truths he repeatedly insisted that this would be the time to ask whatever we wanted and to be assured that our prayers made in his name would be answered. What happens in these brief moments of daily spiritual communion makes a person desire more space and time to penetrate and contemplate these sublime truths at greater length and in ever greater depth. Inevitably a person feels the deep inner pull that is at times clearly tangible, to seek out more space and time to do what we have been created for. And so we experience, in some small measure, what we will one day experience without measure, in our true and everlasting home from home.

Chapter 17

E:
Examination of Conscience

Even though we may make the morning offering as sincerely as possible, and genuinely try to implement it in the forthcoming day, we will ultimately fail unless something is done to cure the scourge of selfishness that can destroy even our best of intentions and our sincerest efforts. God wants us to do all that is within our power to strip away all and everything in our lives that prevents us from being totally united with him at all times. Only then will he be able to possess us as fully as he has planned. If we do not see the sin and the selfishness that prevents our growth in the spiritual life, it is not because we are sinless, it is simply because we are blind and we need to cry out with Bartimaeus, "Master, let me see again." (*Mk* 10:46-52)

In one of the most memorable retreats I have ever attended, Archbishop Anthony Bloom began by telling the story of a retired headmistress who offered her services to him as a chauffeur. As they were returning home one Monday afternoon she stopped the car in Kensington to pick up her new glasses from the opticians and proceeded to try them out for the remainder of the journey. It was less than a mile, but it turned out to be the most terrifying journey either of them ever made. She climbed out of the car shaking all over, opened her handbag, took out her driving licence and ceremoniously ripped it into little pieces. "I'll never drive again," she said. "Why ever not?" asked the Archbishop. "Because," she replied, "there is just so much traffic on the road!" So, if we do not see, it is because we are spiritually blind and need to do something about it.

Whilst working in the Cameroon, I met the holiest man I have ever known. He told me he had been in spiritual darkness for many years. Then, one day he became ill and was admitted to the monastery infirmary where he received Holy Communion each day. On three distinct occasions, just as he was about to receive the host, he heard these words, "Only you have been keeping me out."

We are doing exactly the same and that is why the letter E in the Our Father is to remind us to examine our conscience each day. It is time to ask God to show us everything we have done or failed to do that has kept him out. After this has been done, it is time to make an Act of Contrition for how we have failed in the past. A formal act of contrition could be used, or perhaps the recitation of what came to be called the "Jesus Prayer", said several times over, slowly and prayerfully. "Jesus, son of God, have mercy on me a sinner." But a sincere expression of personal sorrow, in our own words would be better still. Then we could make a firm purpose of amendment, a genuine decision to try and behave better in future. Finally, as we become a little more aware of the moral stumbling blocks that trip us up, it is time to try and forestall them. If there is a lazy streak in us, or if we have a hot temper, or are prone to making unkind remarks at the expense of others, it is time to take the necessary steps to avoid falling into these same faults in the forthcoming day.

St Paul was the first to realise that it is in fact our very weaknesses, and that even includes our sins, that can become stepping stones to sanctity. That is of course if they convince us of our utter need for God. This is good news, because the truth is that in this life we will never stop falling. "When you stop falling you will be in heaven, but when you stop getting up, you will be in hell" (Peter Calvay).

Chapter 18

R:
Repentance

The love that was unleashed by the Risen Christ will never
stop being poured out now and for always, but it will only
be received by those who choose to turn to receive it,
or in the words of St Peter, those who choose to repent.
Every Jew knew what it meant to repent; it meant turning
back to God, for that is what the word repentance meant
throughout the whole of the Old Testament. However, for
Jesus, this traditional word took on a new meaning. For the
first time Jesus, had taught his followers that God was none
other than their ever-loving Dad (*Abba*), and repentance
therefore meant turning back to him. It meant turning back
to the true home where we were all originally conceived,
and to where we will all one day return.

The word *Shub* in Hebrew actually means to return. The
prophet Isaiah uses this word as Jesus was to use it later,
namely of the return of errant sons back to their father.
Jesus came from the home where we were all conceived, to
take us back with him to live with him in a family bonded

together by the love that endlessly surges out of his Father, to enjoy utter, ongoing and ever-increasing joy to all eternity. Many of those who listened to St Peter had an immediate conversion experience. The love that touched the apostles touched them, and they wanted to change their lives immediately. A conversion experience is one thing, but repentance is quite another. Repentance means turning to receive the love that is for ever pouring out of Jesus, not once, but time and time again. How? By relentlessly turning away from all and everything that would impede it, even though this might mean a complete and radical change of life and utter abandonment to God.

Yesterday is gone, tomorrow is to come, so it is only now that a person can turn to God to receive the love that is relentlessly pouring out of him, and into us through Jesus. That is why Jean Pierre de Caussade called the present moment a sacrament, because it is only now that we can abandon ourselves to the love of God. The only way to do this is not by making a grand gesture, as people often do after a conversion experience, but by freely choosing to repent here and now, today and repeatedly every day.

Chapter 19

Morning Prayer

Begin with Psalm sixty-nine with which St Benedict instructed his monks to start the Divine Office. Then it can be followed by the Glory Be, immediately followed by Psalm sixty-two.

O God, come to my aid
O Lord, make haste to help me
Glory be to the Father and to the Son and to the Holy Spirit.
Amen.

O God, you are my God, for you I long;
For you my soul is thirsting.
My body pines for you
Like dry weary land without water.

Say the Our Father and then using the mnemonic "Our Father" as a memory jog, say the following prayers:

O: The Morning Offering
God, our Father, I wish to consecrate all that I say and all that I do to you in this forthcoming day, just as Jesus did every day of his life on earth. Please accept what I do

so imperfectly and unite it with the perfect offering that Jesus continues to make to you in heaven. I offer to you my joys and my sorrows, my successes as well as my failures, because these especially show how much I have need of you. I make my prayer in, with and through Jesus in whom we all live and move and have our being. Amen.

U: <u>U</u>nion

Father, I know that the more your Holy Spirit draws me into your son Jesus, the more I am united to all who are within him. I therefore ask Mary and Joseph, Peter and Paul and all the saints, especially those to whom I have a special devotion, to be with me now as I pray so that my prayers may be fortified by theirs. I also want to pray for all my family and friends, and all who have asked me to pray for them. May they benefit from the day ahead that I wish to make a perfect prayer, as I offer all I say and do to you, through Jesus Christ Our Lord. Amen.

R: <u>R</u>esolutions

Jesus, help me to review the day ahead to anticipate all that I should do, so that I can love God as you did, through everything that I do and love my neighbour too, as you love all of us. Help me to forgive my enemies as you forgave, as well as my friends. And give me the grace to seek forgiveness from those I have offended; and never to cease trying to be like you and to behave like you in all that I say and do. Amen. (Pause to make resolutions for the day ahead.)

Prayer always begins by using many words or prayers, but it always ends up in silence when we begin to experience the love of the One to whom we have been speaking, sometimes to shattering degrees of intensity. Although it may be difficult to begin with, it is essential that we try to cultivate this inner silence so that we may eventually come to experience something of the fullness of love for which we were born. Père Louis Bouyer put it this way: "As vocal prayer is interiorised and purified it goes beyond itself into the prayer of silence which characterises the state of union with God."

Chapter 20

Evening Prayer

F: <u>F</u>aith
Father, I know and believe that you are all loving, and that your love has been permanently transformed into human loving through the human nature of your son, Jesus. I know and believe that his love is perpetually poised to possess me at this moment and at every moment. Penetrate and possess me now, permeate my whole being as I try to turn and remain open to receive you. Melt my heart of stone, re-make it and re-mould it, so that it can at all times be open to receive you. "For I, unless you enthral me, never shall be free, nor ever chaste except you ravish me". (John Donne) Amen.

A: <u>A</u>bandonment
Father, you have freely chosen to share your own inner life and love with me now through Jesus, as a foretaste of the ecstatic joy that you have planned for me and for all who love you in heaven. As there is no limit to the way you have poured out your loving goodness and mercy on me, I can only totally abandon myself to you in return. I therefore solemnly consecrate every moment of every day to you and

to your honour and glory, in and together with your son, Jesus Christ. Amen.

T: Thanksgiving

Father, although you are infinitely distant you are infinitely near too, for you inhabit the inner marrow of my being. I thank you for being with me, and for all you have given me today, for life itself and all and everyone that has made it worth living. Give me the grace to praise, honour and thank you as much as I am able, and more than I am able, not just in words but in a life that I freely dedicate to you. Amen.

H: Holy Communion

Jesus, at the Last Supper you promised to make your home in all who would obey your new commandments. Help me to obey them now and at every moment of my life. For when I love the Father and love my neighbour, as you did, there is nothing to stop you making your home in me and me making mine in you. Let the joy and the peace that comes from abiding in you suffuse all I say and do, so that others may be drawn into the Holy Communion that begins in this life and comes to its completion in the next. Amen.

(Now is the time to remain still and silent for a few moments of contemplation to relish what, or rather whom, we receive in this Holy Communion. A short prayer could be repeated gently whenever distractions threaten to draw the attention elsewhere. A prayer such as "Come, Lord" or "Come, Lord Jesus" would be ideal or another short prayer of your choice.)

E: Examination of Conscience

Lord, that I may see, so that all that prevents you making your home in me may be spirited away. Strengthen me to live the new commandments as you lived them, so that the same Holy Spirit who filled you, guided you and raised you from the dead may do the same for me. Show me the sins that keep you out and give me the power to overcome them, for without you I have no power to do anything. Amen.

R: Repentance

Father, I ask your forgiveness for the sins that have prevented you from possessing me as you would wish this day. (Pause to review our behaviour in the past day.) I am deeply sorry for failing you yet again, and with your grace I will never let my pride cause me to delay from turning back to you the moment I fall. Until I can love everyone as I should, help me to do them no harm and give me the sympathy and compassion of the person in whose footsteps I wish to walk. Amen.

Conclude with an Our Father, a Hail Mary and a Glory Be.

Chapter 21

The Prayer without Ceasing

I never spoke to my father about his or my spiritual life for that matter, but I know that after reading Thomas Merton's autobiography, *Elected Silence*, or *Seven Storey Mountain* as it was first called in the United States, he became very interested in the Desert Fathers. It must have been the way they offered their day and everything in it to God that affected him most.

After his death I found two quotations from John Cassian on the final page of his missal which helped him to keep his morning offering on course throughout the day. The first was a short prayer that my father used whenever he was in need. The prayer was simply, "O God, come to my aid, O Lord, make haste to help me." John Cassian said that the prayer was taught to his disciples by Abbot Isaac and later used by St Benedict with which to begin the Divine Office throughout the day. Under this little prayer my father copied out the second quotation containing the following words from Abbot Isaac, written for the benefit of his followers to help them attain the *prayer without ceasing*:

You must continually use this prayer in your heart, whatever you are doing or whatever office you are holding, or journey you are undertaking; in adversity that you may be delivered, and in prosperity that you may be preserved. You should be so moulded by the constant use of it that when sleep comes you are still considering it so that you become accustomed to repeating it even when you sleep. When you awake let it become the first thing that comes into your mind, let it anticipate all your waking thoughts. When you rise from your bed let it send you down on your knees, and thence send you forth to your work, and let it follow you all through the day.

Abbot Macarius used to tell his disciples to say simply, "Lord, to the rescue," or call upon him by name by using the holy name, Jesus, whenever they were in danger of losing their way or forgetting what they were about. Abbot Macarius was believed to be the originator of the "Jesus Prayer". Later it developed into the prayer, as we know it today, which was originally composed by St John Climacus, "Jesus, Son of God, have mercy on me a sinner." These short prayers were not only used by the Desert Fathers, but have been used continually throughout subsequent centuries. They have always been used to help Christians keep their attention fixed on their calling throughout the day. One of my mother's favourite little prayers that helped her throughout her day was, "Jesus mercy, Mary help."

I remember asking my father why he put little stickers on his wrist watch. One was pointing to nine o'clock, another to twelve o'clock, and the third to three o'clock. He merely said it was a little device to help him remember something. In earlier times when Christian Europe was predominantly rural, the Angelus bell that pealed three times a day, called everyone to prayer wherever they were and whatever they were doing. When it came to his spiritual life my father was an intensely private man who found it difficult to speak about his own journey. However, one thing I know for certain was that he always tried to find some time each day, in addition to all else, to enter into what my mother called his inner garden shed for his daily meditation.

In the next book in this series – *Meditation Made Simple* – I will write about this prayer in some detail.

This series includes:
Prayer Made Simple
Meditation Made Simple
Contemplation Made Simple

The themes contained in this book are expanded more fully in David Torkington's Trilogy:
Wisdom from the Western Isles (the making of an adult Christian)
Wisdom from Franciscan Italy (the example of a perfect Christian)
Wisdom from the Christian Mystics (the making of a perfect Christian)

www.davidtorkington.com

Has this book helped you?

Spread the word!

@CTSpublishers

/CTSpublishers

ctscatholiccompass.org

Let us know!
marketing@ctsbooks.org
+44 (0)207 640 0042

Learn, love, live your faith.
www.CTSbooks.org